BEYOND
THE PAIN

Blessing to you! ♡
Edna Wolfswinkel

BEYOND
THE PAIN

Edna Wolfswinkel

Xulon Press

Xulon Press
2301 Lucien Way #415
Maitland, FL 32751
407.339.4217
www.xulonpress.com

© 2017 by Edna Wolfswinkel

Printed in the United States of America.

Edited by Xulon Press

ISBN-13: 9781545604755

DEDICATION

Thank you to my Children
Dawn, David , Darla and to
Darin (deceased) who gave us many
Wonderful memories!

Acknowledgements

All scripture quotations, unless otherwise indicated are taken from the New King James Version, 1982 by Thomas Nelson, Inc

Scriptures quotations marked Amp are taken from the Amplified Bible, 1987 by the Zondervan Corporation and the Lockman Foundation .

Scriptures quotations marked by KJV are taken from the King James Bible, 1611 by Zondervan Publishing

Scripture quotations marked NIV are taken from the New International Version, 1978 by Tyndale Publishing

TABLE OF CONTENTS

Introduction

This book was written to not dwell on the things that happened to cause the pain but to concentrate on the process of how to deal with pain through our relationship with our Lord Jesus Christ. He took our place on the cross and took the punishment for us.

I believe that God allows circumstances in our lives from which we can grow. In His Word he promises that we will have trials and tribulations but to be of good cheer because He has overcome the world.

We all have problems that are bigger than we can handle. But we also have a God who is bigger than our problems. If we surrender them to Him, He can help us to overcome them. He says to us in Psalm 46:1,2b: God is our Refuge and Strength, a very present help in time of trouble. Therefore we will not fear... We can depend on Him!

My hope is that you can develop this intimate relationship with Him and put the things of the past behind you and move beyond the pain in your life.

Edna Wolfswinkel

CHAPTER 1

LIFE CHANGES

LIFE IS FULL OF EXPERIENCES THAT ARE painful. We cannot escape pain. It is life's best teacher. Life experiences have consequences and some are painful. It also helps us not to repeat some of those experiences.

It is painful to lose someone in death; it is painful to be hurt in an auto accident. Pain is experienced in broken relationships. In each instance you are experiencing pain but in a different way. Sometimes it is pain of the flesh, sometimes pain of the heart and sometimes it's our feelings that feel pain physically. Some pain is good and some is not. Circumstances determine the degree of the pain. Pain from divorce, separation by death, rejection and abusive relationships are all very painful.

On October 12th, 1988 my life changed. I got divorced, and my new life began. I left my home, my church, my friends, my work and started a new life in a new city. I shed lots of tears for what I lost, as it was more painful than I anticipated.

I settled into an apartment that I had rented and started my search for a job. I had lots of time alone since I didn't know very many people in this city. I got to know God as my Provider, best Friend and my Lord, while also getting to know who I was. Waiting for a response after applying for several jobs, I had time to heal from an abusive relationship and divorce. I soon found a job and worked there for about one and a half years. Some time later and a few jobs later, I found my calling, starting a business in therapeutic massage, as working in healthcare was always a dream of mine.

When I started the massage business, I promised God, that the business was His and I would work for

Him. For me, it was a job to earn a living, but a few years later it would become a ministry.

Very early in life, before my massage ministry, I learned the love of my Heavenly Father. I grew up in a home where Mom showed us children, the love of God by demonstrating that love in her own life. Being the second oldest in the family, I was given a lot of responsibilities, as it seemed that babysitting was always my job. There were 12 children in my family. I publicly gave my life to the Lord at age sixteen, but however, I didn't walk faithfully with Him until several years later. It was then that my faith went from my head to my heart!

In March of 1994 I decided to go on a trip to Israel with a group led by a Pastor friend and his wife. It was a dream of mine that I never thought would happen but God made it happen. I received a brochure about the trip in the mail and upon reading it, I desired to go there. I wanted to experience the culture and see the places where Jesus lived His life on this earth.

That night, as I was reading the brochure, God spoke to my heart for I felt Him say, "I want you to go". My heart skipped a beat. Could it be? Again I heard Him say, "I want you to go".

The following day, the county recorder came in for a massage appointment. I asked her what I would have to do to get a passport. She told me to come to her office bringing my drivers license and birth certificate with me. She told me that some of the government offices were shut down due to budget problems, so it could take a long time to get the passport. I knew that if God told me He wanted me to go, He would work it out so that the passport would arrive in time. The passport came about three weeks later, and I was scheduled to leave in about six weeks.

The trip was all I hoped for, and more. We went to the places that the Bible talks about. We walked the paths that Jesus walked and saw the places where He ministered.

We went to the upper room, where we had a praise and worship service, and then went to the place where he preached the Sermon on the Mount.

We went to the city of Nazareth, where he grew up as a young child. We went to Capernaum where Jesus healed Peter's mother-in-law and to where He taught in the synagogue.

We also went to the Antonia Fortress where the trial of Jesus was held.

We went to the tomb and saw that it was empty! As I stood in the tomb, I felt the pain of sorrow and the joy of the resurrection all at the same time!

We went to the Mt. Of Olives and the Garden of Gethsemane, where Jesus spent time with His disciples and where He sweat great drops of blood, while taking upon Himself all of our sins.

We went for a boat ride on the Sea of Galilee and had a service on the boat. I felt so privileged to experience the culture where Jesus lived on this earth.

We also went to the Jezreel Valley, where the Bible says the war of Armagedon will be fought. As I stood on the place where King Solomon's palace was, I looked all around and could see the whole valley. It was an amazing feeling to know that I stood on the place of the past, the present and the future. What an awesome experience. Praise God!

It was there that I asked the Pastor if I could be baptized. He said, "Certainly". He took us to the Jordon River where I was baptized. I had been sprinkled as a baby, but the Bible says in Mark 16:16, NKJV, "He who believes and is baptized will be saved". I wanted to do this as an adult because I made the choice to follow Jesus. What awesome experience! The Pastor explained how the water represented the grave and how the old man is buried and we are raised to new life in Christ unto His resurrection. The Bible says in Second Corinthians 5:17, NKJV, "Therefore, if anyone is in Christ, he is a new creation; old things have passed away; behold all things have become new". I was now a new creature in Christ Jesus.

It was such an awesome experience to see the river flowing. All my old life from that moment flowed down the river with the current. All the garbage from my past was gone. I felt so clean; that's when my life began to change.

The Bible says in Acts 1:8, "when the Holy Spirit comes upon you, you will receive power and you will be My witnesses…"I came back from Israel a different person and was no longer afraid to talk about Jesus.

I believe that God called me to minister healing to the sick and hurting people. I also believe that God allowed many hurtful experiences in my life so that I could identify with others who are experiencing similar things in their lives. I promised God that if anyone were walking the same path I walked, he/she would not have to walk that path alone. God is so good! God used me so many times to be a blessing to people that I was able to work with over the years.

I'm reminded of one time when my son was in the hospital. It was a time that my husband and I were separated and contemplating divorce, and my son had been diagnosed with a Wilms tumor, which was cancerous. We had been told that day that his cancer was terminal, and my husband and I were both present in the room.

My son was in so much pain. I left the room to cry; for I didn't want to cry in his presence because he would get upset, so I went to the bathroom. I cried out and said, "God, I can't take any more. My marriage is broke, my parents disowned me and my son is dying"! My heart was broken.

After a time collecting myself, I came back into the room. My husband was standing on the opposite side of the bed from me. As I stood there, someone entered the room. He looked familiar and yet different. He came and stood in front of me, took my hands into his, looked into my eyes and said "I'm here to deliver a message from God". 'Be still and know that I am God' from Psalm 46:10". Then the man left without saying another word. I don't know if my husband or son saw him, as we never spoke to each other about it. I knew that it was a message from God.

I had heard that verse many times before, but it never meant more to me than it meant to me right then. I stood in awe! God had heard and answered my prayer. He sent an angel to deliver His message to me personally. I'll never forget those blue eyes of the man; it was as if they looked right through me. I knew then that God was in control and I needed to trust Him. He would take care of everything. How awesome is that! My son passed away a few months later but somehow, by God's grace, I found the strength to grow through this traumatic experience. The Word says in First Peter 5:7,NKJV, ' to cast all our cares on Him for He cares for you'. I needed to do that, give my cares to Him.

First Peter 5:10 says, "But the God of all grace, who called us to His eternal glory by Christ Jesus, after you have suffered a while, perfect, establish, strengthen and settle you. To Him be the glory and dominion forever and ever". Amen.

God promises to strengthen us. What a comfort that is in knowing!

CHAPTER 2

LETTING GO

ONE EVENING IN 1971, MY HUSBAND AND I went to a Lay Witness meeting at our church, held by a group of people who we called "Jesus people". I have to say that we went out of curiosity sitting in the back pew with our friends. We planned to leave if things got weird. After a praise and worship service and listening to some testimonies, we were broken apart into separate groups. They started numbering in the back row so we could hardly leave now.

The leader in my group posed a question to us; are you willing to let go and let God? I felt as if she posed that question directly to me. I asked her to finish the question. "Let go and let God what?"She said that I should think about that. I pondered that question all that night and the next day.

I finally asked God, "Let you what? What do you want?" I felt God spoke to my heart and said, "I want all of you". I replied, "You have all of me". He said, "No, I don't have your closets". I said, "You can't have my closets". (My closets were my private places in my heart.) "I need them for times when my husband and I go places that you may not approve of". Then He said something that really touched me deeply. He said "If I can't have your closets, then I don't want any part of you because I will have to hold you responsible for willfully sinning". I was devastated!

First John 3:9, NIV tells us: "No one who is born of God will continue to sin, because God's seed remains in him; he cannot go on sinning, because he has been born of God".

I told Him that I had tried to be a good wife: I tried to be a good mother; I tried to be a good daughter; I tried to be a good Christian; didn't that count for something? I then became aware of all the I's in my conversation. There was too much of me and not enough of Him.

Suddenly, I remembered that I had promised God that I would be a missionary nurse when I grew up. Somehow I thought He was holding me to that promise. I told Him that I was now married and that I had children and I was not able to go to distant lands and fulfill that promise; as if He didn't know that!

I struggled all afternoon, and finally told God that I would do whatever He wanted me to do and go wherever He wanted me to go. I surrendered all my closets and gave Him all that I am and all that I'm not. When I did that, a peace came over me, as I had never experienced before. He gives us a peace that surpasses all understanding. No, I didn't have to leave my family and go to a distant land; my mission was at home.

After that, I became so hungry for a deeper under-standing of the Word; I just couldn't get enough of

God's Word. I fell in love with the book of James, as it spoke to me as never before. I believe it was God's way of preparing me for all the hurtful experiences that were ahead of me. It was after that experience that many hurtful things happened. My youngest son got cancer and passed away, my parents disowned me because my father disagreed with some of my decisions, and my marriage fell apart. Life dealt me some very hard blows, but God was my only stability. He became my best friend. Life is not always fair, but God never promised that it would be fair. Jesus promised that we would have trials.

In John 16:33, AMP, it says,

I have told you these things, so that in Me you may have peace and confidence. In the world you have tribulation and trials and distress and frustration; but be of good cheer, for I have overcome the world.

With Him all things are possible!

I like what Hebrews 13:5, AMP says,

I will not in any way fail you nor give you up, nor leave you without support. [I will] not, [I will] not, [I will] not in any degree leave you helpless, nor forsake, nor let [you] down. [Relax my hold on you.] [most assuredly not].

Isaiah 61:7, AMP says,

Instead of your former shame, you shall have a two fold recompense, instead of dishonor and reproach, your people shall rejoice in their portion. Therefore in their land they shall possess double what they had forfeited [everlasting joy shall be theirs].

I claim that promise! God's Word is so comforting. I believe that God will replace all that Satan has stolen from us.

Paul says in Philippians 3:13-14,

Forgetting what lies behind and straining forward to what lies ahead, I press on toward the goal to win the prize to which God in Christ Jesus is calling us upward.

We need to put the past behind us and press on to what's ahead. We can't move forward until we let go of the past; you must understand that only by God's grace can we do this. We have the confidence that He never asks us to do what He does not equip us to do.

CHAPTER 3

EXPERIENCES

I BELIEVE THAT GOD ALLOWED ME TO USE the previous mentioned experiences to minister to hurting people as follows;

After I opened my Massage Therapy business, a man came in to my office for massage therapy. He shared a lot of things from his life, some of them good and some not so good. He said he had problems with sexual thoughts. He also said he was married but that he was not satisfied and confessed to being a Christian. I asked him what having these sexual thoughts did to his marriage, which he said he tried not to think about that. I also asked him what this did to his relationship with God, but he said he hadn't thought much about that either. I reminded him of what price Christ paid for his sin; that he needed to confess his sin and ask God for forgiveness for what he was thinking. It really didn't seem to sink in until after he was diagnosed with cancer.

We continued to talk and I continued to pray with him both for him to recognize his sin and for healing from the cancer. After a time, he confessed his sin and asked God for forgiveness. Before he died he came in and thanked me for not giving up on him and for continuing to pray for him. It is so rewarding to know that he is now spending eternity with his Lord.

Another man who also had cancer came in to my office for massage therapy. A friend of his came and told me that he was not a Christian and that he had tried to share the gospel with him; however, he did not want to talk about it. I prayed for God to give me a chance to talk to him.

A few weeks later he called for an appointment. While doing the massage, I prayed for wisdom in how to share the gospel with him. After the massage was completed, I asked him if I could pray with him. He sighed and said "Okay". In the prayer, God laid it upon my heart to present the plan of salvation. I knew He didn't like confrontation, so this was perfect.

He sat down in the office after the massage and we talked. I talked with him about my son also having cancer, sharing with him about the faith of my son who was five years old. He loved God and shared his faith so willingly. The man sat and listened intently. I told him that God was giving him time to set his house in order, but not everyone gets time to do that. I shared with him that the best is yet to come if we commit our lives to God.

After a time he left, and a few weeks later he called and asked for another appointment. Again, I did the massage and again I asked him if I could pray for him. He said, "Please do". When I finished praying, he said, "Amen, Amen!" I knew he had made a decision for Christ. That was the last time I saw him; he died a short time later.

Working in massage therapy is such a wonderful privilege. People talk about problems that are stressful to them. Massage therapy helps to treat physical, emotional and mental problems. It opens up opportunities to share Jesus with them.

Another day a man came into my office. He was in so much pain that he could hardly move, even when walking with crutches. I told him that I was not a doctor, but he said someone had sent him here and he wanted me to work on him. For an hour I worked on his back, and then told him that I had done all I could do for that day. Then I asked him if I could anoint him with oil, lay hands on him and pray. He said he would love that.

When I prayed, I felt the power of God so strong in that room; it was overwhelming. I left the room after the prayer and waited for him in the office. When he came out of the room, he threw his hands in the air and said "Praise God, I'm healed"! He left carrying his crutches in his hands. The next few days he told everyone he knew how God had healed him. God is so good. God is still in the business of healing today.

John 3:16, NKJV, says

For God so loved the world that He gave His only begotten Son, that whoever believes in him should not perish, but have everlasting life.

Jesus sacrificed everything for us! Can we do less than surrender our lives to Him and make Him Lord of our lives?

Paul says, in Philippians 3:10-11, AMP [For my determined purpose is] that I may *know Him* [that I may progressively become more deeply and intimately acquainted with Him, perceiving and recognizing and understanding the wonders of His Person more strongly and more clearly], and that I may in that same way come to know the power out flowing from His resurrection [which it exerts over believers], and that I may so share His sufferings as to be continually trans-formed [in spirit and into His likeness even] to His death, [in the hope] that if possible I may attain to the [spiritual and moral] resurrection [that lifts me] out from among the dead [even while in the body]. (Emphasis mine)

We can only know Him if we study His Word and have a personal relationship with Him! The more you get to know Him, the more you will become like Him. Most people don't understand what it means to sacrifice their life for someone else. We are usually not asked to do that. Jesus paid for our sins by dying on the cross. What a horrible way to die and He did that for us, you and me. He took our place so that we could enjoy eternal life with Him at His place!

CHAPTER 4

MY PROVIDER

MANY TIMES I HAVE BEEN CONCERNED about how I would make ends meet financially. I have had to walk by faith and not by sight.

Being a single person and self- employed is not easy. As I said before, God has become my best friend; I have learned to depend on Him.

Isaiah 54:5, AMP, says "For your Maker is your husband, the Lord of hosts is His name; and the Holy One of Israel is your Redeemer; the God of the whole earth He is called".

I recall a time when my car broke down on my way home. The transmission went out which left me stranded thirty miles from home. I called a tow truck to pull me home.

The next day I called some mechanics and they quoted what it would cost to get the transmission fixed. I had a limited amount of money set aside for "a rainy day", but all the estimates that I received were much higher than what I had set aside. I went to my knees and prayed. "God, how can I pay for this?"

The next few days, I expected something to appear in the mail or someone would remember me in his or her will. Well, that didn't happen!

My brother was an auto mechanic and agreed to fix my car for less than some of the quotes I received. When the car was finished, we met for dinner. After we had eaten, he asked how I would like to pay the bill. I breathed a prayer and God spoke to my heart and said to give him a check.

By now I knew that when God speaks, I listen. I gave him a check for the full amount. Again I breathed a prayer and said, "Ok, God, I did what you asked; now it's up to you".

The following day, I received my bank statement in the mail. There was enough money in the bank to cover that check and some extra. I checked to be sure I entered all the right numbers and could not find any errors. I don't understand how God does what He does, but I trust Him! I am comforted to know that God's promises are true; we can depend on Him.

Matthew 6:25-34 says:

Therefore I say to you, do not worry about your life, what you will eat or what you will drink; nor about your body, what you will put on. Is not life more than food and the body more than clothing? Look at the birds of the air, for they neither sow nor reap nor gather into barns; yet your heavenly Father feeds them. Are you not of more value than they? Which of you by worrying can add one cubit to his stature? So why do you worry about clothing? Consider the lilies of the field, how they grow: they neither toil nor spin; and yet you say that even Solomon in all his glory was not arrayed like one of these? Now if God so clothes the grass of the field, which today is, and tomorrow is thrown into the oven, will He not much more clothe you, O you of little faith?

Therefore do not worry, saying, what shall we eat? Or what shall we drink? Or what shall we wear? For after all these things the Gentiles seek. For your heavenly Father knows that you need all these things. But seek first the kingdom of God and His righteousness, and all these things shall be added to you. Therefore do not worry about tomorrow, for tomorrow will worry about its own things. Sufficient for the day is its own trouble.

There are times when we have silent years; times when we feel that God does not hear us. I believe that in those times, God is doing a deep work in us. Many of the characters in the Bible also had those silent times.

I think of Abraham, when God promised him that He would make him a great nation. He waited until he was one hundred years old to give him the promised son. Also Moses, spent forty years in the wilderness tending sheep before God called him to deliver the children of Israel from Egypt; or of Joseph, when he was in jail for several years before God promoted him to second in command to Pharaoh. The time between the Old and New Testaments was four hundred years when it seemed God was silent from speaking to the prophets as He had done before.

I believe that these are times that God is preparing us for what God has planned for the days ahead.

Isaiah 26:3, says, "You will keep him in perfect peace, whose mind is stayed on You, because he trusts in you".

What a comfort to know that God is in control.

CHAPTER 5

GOD'S PLANS

"I KNOW THE PLANS I HAVE FOR YOU", declares the Lord , "plans to prosper you and not to harm you, plans to give you a hope and a future". Jeremiah. 29:11, NIV

One day a seventy four year old man came into my office for an appointment. As I was working with him, he started to cry. I asked him why he was crying, which he said, "I have no reason to live anymore". He told me that he had many surgeries and that his wife had passed away that same year; he lost his will to live.

I told him that obviously God was not finished with him, since he was still here. I asked him some questions about whether he had any hobbies or things he liked to do. He said yes, that he liked to sing. He sang for a lot of weddings, funerals and other occasions.

So I gave him an assignment before he came back for the next appointment. I suggested that he record a tape of his singing and bring it back with him the next time he came in for a massage; he did just that.

I listened to the tape and was impressed by the richness of his voice. I told him that his singing was beautiful, and that he should make some recordings of his music. He said that he had looked into that, but that he would have to order one thousand tapes. What would he do with all those tapes! I suggested that he should contact the nursing homes, churches and organizations in the area, and offer to do programs for them.

After a few weeks, he came back and said that he had done what I had suggested. He had a couple of programs lined up. I kept encouraging him and within a short time he was so busy that he was traveling three states regularly to give programs. He also ordered the tapes, selling some and giving some to people he ministered to at events. He also recorded a second tape.

Some time later, the local TV station featured him on the news as the "Singing Senior". Also the local paper featured him on the front page as the "Singing Senior". He had a new lease on life!

God had a plan for him. He needed some encouragement, and he needed to be obedient to follow God's plan. "A man's heart plans his way but the Lord directs his steps". (Proverbs 16: 9).

God has a plan for each of us; we need to seek His will for our lives. God has given to each of us gifts to use for His service; singing is one of those gifts.

Chapter 6

The Enemy

Satan comes against us in many ways.

First Peter 5:8,9 says,

> Be of sober spirit, be vigilant; because your adversary the devil walks about like a roaring lion, seeking whom he may devour. Resist him, steadfast in the faith, knowing that the same sufferings are experienced by your brotherhood in the world.

He tries to destroy our lives by lying to us. He tells us that God will not be there for you. God does not love you. God can't use you. You are a sinner and He can't forgive you. Satan will try to beat you down so that you feel you can't do anything worthwhile. But,

God, God is faithful. He is greater and more powerful than the prince of this world.

First John 4:4, NKJV, says, "You are of God, little children, and have overcome them, because He who is in you is greater than He who is in the world".

Romans 8:28, NKJV also says, "And we know that all things work together for good to those who love God and are called according to His purpose". We need to quote Scripture back to Satan.

Romans 8:37 NIV says, "No, in all these things we are more than conquerors through him who loved us". We can be victorious over Satan and his demons!

Romans 8:11 says , "But if the Spirit of Him who raised Jesus from the dead dwells in you, He who raised Christ from the dead will also give life to your mortal bodies through His Spirit who dwells in you".

Praise God! The Spirit of God lives in me. We need to claim the power that is given to us by the Holy Spirit! We need to walk by faith and not by sight.

Act 10:38 says "and how God anointed Jesus of Nazareth with the Holy Spirit and power, and how He went about doing good and healing all who were oppressed by the devil, for God was with Him".

If we will believe, He will give us faith and equip us to do His will. God never asks us to do something that He doesn't give us the ability to do.

Act 1:8 says, "But you shall receive power when the Holy Spirit comes upon you and you will be My witnesses in Jerusalem, and in all Judea and Samaria to the ends of the earth".

This scripture verse means to minister or witness to those who live around us. To me Samaria, means to minister to those we are not comfortable with. The Jews were not to go through Samaria. The Jews hated Samaritans. It was not comfortable for them to go through that area, but Jesus did. So we, too, need to get out of our comfort zones. God has called us to be His ambassadors.

Second Corinthians 5:20, NIV states, "We are therefore Christ's ambassadors, as God were making His appeal through us".

God has anointed us to do what He has called us to do. He wants us to serve Him with passion and with our whole heart!

First John 2:20, AMP, says: "But you have been anointed by [you hold a sacred appointment from, you have been given an unction from] the Holy One, and you know [the Truth] or you know all things."

Verse 27 says "As for you, the anointing you received from Him remains in you, [abides in you] and you do not need anyone to teach you. But as His anointing teaches you about all things and as that anointing is real, not counterfeit – just as it has taught you, remain in Him".

Abiding means that it will not leave us. God will show us what He has anointed us to do in this life.

John 14:12-14, "Most assuredly, I say to you, he who believes in Me, the works that I do he will do also;

and greater works than these he will do, because I go to My Father. And whatever you ask in My name, that I will do, that the Father may be glorified in the Son, If you ask anything in My name, I will do it."

What a promise; Jesus is all about bringing glory to the Father. Think of the power that gives you and me. Second Corinthians 5:21, NKJV, says, "For He made Him who knew no sin to be sin for us, that we might become the righteousness of God in Him". How awesome is that! God trusts us to be His representatives to people around us.

Second Corinthians 2:14,15, AMP says: "But thanks be to God, who in Christ always leads us in triumph [as trophies of Christ's victory] and through us spreads and makes evident the fragrance of the knowledge of God everywhere. For we are the sweet fragrance of Christ [which exhales] unto God, [discernible alike] among those who are being saved and among those who are perishing".

CHAPTER 7

REJECTION

REJECTION IS ANOTHER TYPE OF PAIN: being rejected by parents, peers, children and/or spouses are all very painful. The Bible also describes it as forsaken.

Psalm 27:9,10, NIV says, "Do not hide your face from me, do not turn your servant away in anger, you have been my helper. Do not reject me or forsake me, O God my Savior. Though my father and mother forsake me, the Lord will receive me".

God is very faithful and loves His people.

Hebrews 13:5b, NIV says, "Never will I leave you; never will I forsake you".

In 1988, my husband and I divorced; I felt so rejected. It was so painful because I had invested so much of my life into my marriage. We were blessed with four children and experienced the death of our youngest son together. We still had three children, two girls and one boy. They were adults but still needed parents. I felt that twenty three and half years of marriage died with the divorce. It felt like it was a death because it was over; it was finished. It couldn't be revived. The pain was real. I had to go through the mourning stage, the anger stage and the acceptance stage and then get on with my life, somehow alone. I was scared. I needed to find a job in a new place.

I needed to find a new place to live and moved to a new city for a fresh start. Starting my life over at midlife was a challenge. Again, I called on God for my help, because without Him, I couldn't do this! I claimed God's promises.

Philippians. 4:19, NIV explains, "My God shall meet all your needs according to His glorious riches in Christ Jesus".

When my youngest son passed away, it was devastating. Separation by death is very painful. Nothing I could do would bring him back. Again, I needed to go through the stages of mourning, anger, acceptance and getting on with my life without him, but God was my comfort! Without Him, I couldn't do this. Only by God's grace could I go on with my life.

Second Corinthians 12:9, NIV says, "My grace is sufficient for you, for my power is made perfect in weakness."God is a God of comfort in our times of weakness.

There is also physical pain when you injure you body, which I had. Sometime ago, I fell and hurt my back. The pain was excruciating, to where I needed to go to the emergency room for treatment and then needed to take time to recuperate. I missed several days of work and couldn't attend some of the activities that I had scheduled. I needed time to heal, but God is also a healer for physical pain. What a God! God understands and feels our pain.

Isaiah 53:3 says, "He was despised and rejected by men, a man of sorrows and familiar with suffering. Like one from whom men hide their faces and He was despised, and we esteemed Him not."

He suffered the pain of humiliation and was crucified on the cross; it doesn't get more painful than that! He feels the pain of rejection each time we reject Him or deny Him. He so desires for us to have an intimate relationship with Him, for He is the creator of relationships!

Zephaniah 3:17b, NIV says, "He will take great delight in you, He will quiet you with His love, He will rejoice over you with singing.

Isaiah 49:16, NIV says, "See, I have engraved you on the palms of my hands;"That's how much He loves you!

John 3:16 says, "For God so loved the world, that He gave His only begotten Son, that whosoever believes in Him should not perish but have everlasting life". God is awesome!

There are many more painful situations in my life that I could write about, but rather than dwelling on the situations, I want to dwell on the fact that God is bigger than any situation we can experience. There is life beyond the pain! God has made it very plain in His Word that we will have trials and tribulations, but be of good cheer, I have overcome the world. (John 16:33)

CHAPTER 8

GOD OF MIRACLE

AFTER TWENTY-TWO YEARS OF LIVING IN the same city, I decided to move to another city to be closer to my family. I sold my Massage Therapy business and left town. I felt it was what God wanted me to do. It was very hard to leave a city where I had established myself in business. I was very involved in the different boards of the city and more. I left my home, my friends, my business, my church, and everything that was dear to me. However, I felt God calling me to a new mission field.

In this new city, I tried to reestablish my massage business, it was very slow and didn't seem to grow. I asked God many times, "why did you want me to move here?" It was a long winter season, so I really questioned my move.

After some time, I told Him that I was willing to change jobs if He was finished with me doing ministry through massage therapy. I would do whatever He wanted me to do. I surrendered my will to His, and started looking for a different job.

One night, I was looking at my email. I noticed an email that I did not recognize but opened it up; it was a devotional. As I read it, I noticed a link on the side that read "Jobs for Christians". I opened it up. I scrolled down to find out what kind of jobs was listed. It was churches looking for music directors, education chairpersons, etc. Suddenly I saw the name of the Christian bookstore in the town where I was living. Wow! I could hardly believe it. I never thought of applying there, so I immediately updated my resume. I brought it in to the store the next morning. They told me the owner would not be in until the next week. I told her that was fine and just have her call me when she came into the store.

She called the next week and asked me to come in so she could talk with me. When I came in, she, her husband

and I went to a quiet place and talked. She asked me what kind of job I was looking for, which I told her that I saw the ad online and was applying for whatever they had available. She got this puzzled look on her face and asked her husband if he had listed a job. He said "No, did you?" She said "No". Then she turned to me and asked where I had seen the ad. I told her I had seen it online.

I couldn't remember exactly what the website was, but it said that they had a part time job open. She said that they had not listed a job although one of their employees was quitting the next day. They had agreed to pray that God would send the right person. I replied, "Well, here I am," to which we all laughed.

We then talked about the wages, and the owner told me that she would get back to me within hours. I started work the next week. Later, I went back to the website with the job listings and it was no longer there. How awesome is God! God did have other plans for me! I loved the job and the people I worked with, working at the store for four and a half years. The job ended when the business was sold.

Sometime later, I started having a persistant pain in my side. I went to the doctor, who took blood tests, ordered a CT scan, which showed nothing. He also took X-rays to check vertebrae and disc problems. Everything checked out fine. So a colonoscopy was ordered. Results showed a tumor, which the doctor said was cancerous. He ordered more tests, including another CT scan with iodine contrast to check organs around the site to make sure the cancer had not spread. Then he ordered another colonoscopy to take more biopsies.

I decided to go to a gastrologist to have the second one done. In the meantime, many people were praying for me. It was a time a lot of thoughts went through my mind; I was scared! I went to have the second colonoscopy. When the doctor was finished, he came in and talked to me. He said he found no cancer or anything that looked like cancer! He took more biopsies, which all came back clean! I was on cloud nine and was so happy! I praised God for His healing power! What a God we serve.

God has healed me many times in the past, for God is so good. God is still in the business of healing. He is all powerful. God is the same yesterday, today and forever.

A few months later I moved to a new apartment. There I met a man who had a bone infection and had doctored with that for eight years. Anything they tried didn't help. He wore a brace on the ankle, and it was twice its normal size. I was told that they had prayer meetings at the apartment so I invited him to come to the prayer meeting. I told him that we would like to pray for healing for his ankle. When he came the group stood around him and laid hands on him and I led in prayer with my hands on his ankle. We prayed that God would heal his ankle and that he would be allowed to walk normally. He was so touched by that.

A week or so later he came to my door and thanked me for praying for him. Then he showed me his ankle and it was totally healed. The skin was all nice and pink instead of purple as it had been. It was normal size and he didn't need to wear a brace anymore. God is so good. He is our Healer!

I also want to add that God healed my relationship with my parents after twelve years of being estranged from the family.

It has been such a privilege to serve God in the different avenues God has presented in my life. He is an awesome God! He has taken care of me physically, spiritually, emotionally and mentally. He is my source of strength and He is my joy!

Because of my training and education, I'm privileged to pray and counsel with hurting people. God expects us to minister where we live, for we are to be like Jesus. He is our example. We are not to compare ourselves with anyone else, but we are to strive to be like Him. The only way we can do that is to spend time with Him and be in His Word!

Ephesians 3:16-20, NIV says:

"I pray that out of His glorious riches He may strengthen you with power through His Spirit in your inner being, so that Christ may dwell in your hearts through faith. And I pray that you, being rooted and established in love, may have power, together with all the saints, to grasp how wide and long and high and deep is the love of Christ, and to know this love that surpasses knowledge, that you may be filled to the measure, of all the fullness of God. Now to Him who is able to do immeasurably more than all we ask or imagine, according to His power that is at work within us to Him be glory in the church and in Christ Jesus throughout all generations, forever and ever. Amen".

May this book give you hope in whatever situation you find yourself. My prayer is that if you don't know Jesus as your personal Savior that you will ask Him into your heart right now.

Jeremiah 29:12-14, AMP says,

"Then you will call upon Me, and you will come and pray to Me and I will hear and heed you. Then you will seek Me, inquire for, and require Me [as a vital necessity] and find Me when you search for Me with all your heart".

Deuteronomy 4:29-30 says,

"But from there you will seek the Lord your God, and you will find Him if you search for Him with all you heart and all your soul".

I pray that you will grow in the grace and knowledge of our Lord and Savior Jesus Christ. The Bible says "Today is the day of salvation"! Don't let anything keep you from making the greatest decision of your life. STEP OUT AND MAKE A STAND FOR CHRIST!

God bless you!
Edna Wolfswinkel

About the Author

Edna Wolfswinkel lives in Alexandria, Minnesota. She is privileged to be the mother of three children, five grandchildren, and three great grandchildren. She was a Massage Therapist for the past twenty five years. She also worked in The Mustard Seed Christian Book Store in Alexandria, Minnesota for four and a half years, until it was sold. She lived through many painful experiences in her life. Her hope is that this book will help many people to find hope and healing from their own painful experiences.

CPSIA information can be obtained
at www.ICGtesting.com
Printed in the USA
FFOW05n0024160717

9 781545 604755